Wildebeests

Wildebeests

Sharon Sharth

THE CHILD'S WORLD®, INC.

Published in the United States of America by The Child's World®, Inc.
PO Box 326
Chanhassen, MN 55317-0326
800-599-READ
www.childsworld.com

Product Manager Mary Berendes
Editor Katherine Stevenson
Designer Mary Berendes
Contributor Bob Temple

Photo Credits
ANIMALS ANIMALS © A. & M. Shah: 9
© Ann & Rob Simpson: 30
© Charles V. Angelo, The National Audubon Society Collection/Photo Researchers: 19
© 1992 Craig Brandt: cover
© 1995 Craig Brandt: 16
© Gregory G. Dimijian, The National Audubon Society Collection/Photo Researchers: 24
© Joe McDonald/Visuals Unlimited: 26
© Karl H. Switak, The National Audubon Society Collection/Photo Researchers: 6
© 2001 Manoj Shah/Stone: 29
© 2001 Mark Petersen/Stone: 20
© 1995 Mike Barlow/Dembinsky Photo Assoc. Inc.: 15
© Nigel J. Dennis, The National Audubon Society Collection/Photo Researchers: 13
© 1994 Stan Osolinski/Dembinsky Photo Assoc. Inc.: 10
© Stephen J. Krasemann, The National Audubon Society Collection/Photo Researchers: 23
© 2000 Wendy Dennis/Dembinsky Photo Assoc. Inc.: 2

Library of Congress Cataloging-in-Publication Data
Sharth, Sharon.
Wildebeests / by Sharon Sharth.
p. cm.
ISBN 1-56766-882-8 (lib. bdg. : alk. paper)
1. Gnus—Juvenile literature. [1. Gnus.] I. Title.
QL737.U53 S47 2000
599.64'59—dc21
00-010998

On the cover...

Front cover: This male blue wildebeest has mud on his face from rolling on the ground.
Page 2: This blue wildebeest is drinking from a water hole in South Africa.

Table of Contents

The morning sun heats up the African plains. Surrounded by others of its kind, a large gray animal paws at the dusty ground. It plops down and wriggles its body in the dirt. The rest of the group gallops away. The ground shakes from the stampede. Like a shot, the animal jumps up and races after them, leaping over anything in its path. What is this speedy creature? It's a wildebeest!

⇐ This blue wildebeest is taking a "dust bath." It is rolling in the dirt to get rid of bugs that are making it itch.

What Are Wildebeests?

Wildebeests (pronounced WILL-deh-beests) are large African antelopes. Another name for the wildebeest is the "gnu" (NOO). They are often called gnus because of the noise they make. Like dogs, people, and many other animals, wildebeests are **mammals.** Mammals are animals that grow hair and feed their babies milk from their mothers.

This adult blue wildebeest lives in Kenya. ⇒

What Do Wildebeests Look Like?

Imagine body parts from different animals all scrambled together to make a new creature. That's what a wildebeest looks like! It has a horse's mane and tail and a beard like a goat. It has a buffalo's humped back, a mule's short neck, and a cow's long black face. Its thin legs and **hooves** are like those of a deer. But this strange mixture of parts dances and leaps as gracefully as any antelope! Both male and female wildebeests have smooth, pointy, ox-like horns that curl up toward the sky.

⬅ This blue wildebeest is drinking from a puddle in South Africa.

Are There Different Kinds of Wildebeests?

There are two different kinds of wildebeests. *Blue wildebeests,* also called *brindled wildebeests,* are up to eight feet long from their heads to their tails. They can weigh over 400 pounds. Their coats are bluish gray, and dark brown lines wind around their bodies. Most have black tails, manes, and beards. Some have white beards. There are probably over 1.5 million of these wildebeests in the wild. That is the largest population of wild grazing mammals left in the world!

Black wildebeests (also called *white-tailed wildebeests*) are smaller animals. They are **extinct** in the wild. Happily, their numbers are increasing now that they are protected in zoos and parks.

Here you can see a black wildebeest as it runs in a national park. ⇒

What Do Wildebeests Eat?

Wildebeests are plant-eaters. They usually eat grass—lots of grass! And they eat all the time. They spend most of each day grazing on young, short, tender shoots. In the wild, they share their food with zebras, which prefer taller, coarser grass. Wildebeests also share the land with Thompson's gazelles, which nibble on the tiny bits of grass the wildebeests leave behind.

Wildebeests live in large groups called **herds.** When the herd devours all the grass, or when the hot sun makes the grass too dry, the herd must move on to greener pastures.

This blue wildebeest is grazing on grasses in Kenya. ⇒

Wildebeests live on the grasslands of Africa, in both flat and hilly areas. They are also a common sight in Africa's wildlife parks, or **refuges**.

Wildebeests prefer grassy plains near water. During the dry season, they escape to the woods. In the woods, shade from the trees helps keep the grass from drying out. Some wildebeest herds remain in one area the whole year, if food and water are plentiful. Other herds move, or **migrate,** to find food and water.

⇐ These blue wildebeests are grazing along with a herd of zebras in Kenya.

Why Do Wildebeests Migrate?

For over a million years, wildebeests have traveled across the African plains to find water and fresh grass. Today, hundreds of thousands of wildebeests join together for a 300-mile migration that never really ends. They chase the rain from the south to the north and back again. Rain makes the grasses grow, and the wildebeests must have green grass to eat. They migrate to survive.

Here you can see part of a huge herd of blue ⇒ wildebeests during their migration in Kenya.

Wildebeests always seem to be in a hurry! They thunder across the plains to catch the last drops of rainwater and nibble on the first green grasses. Their migration is one of the longest and most dangerous migrations of grazing mammals in the world. On this journey they cross raging rivers and lakes, have babies, and protect their young.

⇐ These blue wildebeests are hurrying to cross the Mara River during their migration.

What Are Baby Wildebeests Like?

All baby wildebeests, or **calves,** are born during the same few weeks of the year. Hundreds of thousands of calves are born almost at the same time. Each reddish brown newborn stands up when it is only a few minutes old. The mother licks the calf and steadies it on its feet. She helps it get ready to run with her as soon as possible. The newborn usually joins the migrating herd less than 10 minutes after birth!

A wildebeest calf must stick close to its mother at all times. If left alone, it becomes an easy meal for lions or hyenas. Having many calves born at the same time helps make sure that most of them will survive.

Here a mother wildebeest cares for her newborn calf. The calf ⇒ learned to stand just seconds before this picture was taken.

How Do Wildebeests Stay Safe?

Wildebeests know that there is safety in numbers. That is why so many wildebeests travel together in one huge group. Hundreds of wildebeests graze at the same time, move at the same speed, and give birth at about the same time. A wildebeest separated from the herd has little chance of surviving in the wild.

⇐ These two females have had babies at the same time. Each mother knows her calf by its smell.

Many animals stalk and eat wildebeests. Lions are the biggest threat. They and other hunters, or **predators,** follow the herd and pounce when they get the chance. Hyenas, cheetahs, and wild dogs hunt in packs or in pairs to bring down sickly or young wildebeests. Small jackals are always on the lookout for young calves. Sometimes humans illegally kill wildebeests for their meat.

⇐ Here a cheetah is attacking an adult blue wildebeest. The wildebeest has put its head down and is trying to defend itself with its horns.

Every year, wildebeests in the Serengeti Park must cross the deep, swirling Mara River. Some wildebeests drown when impatient wildebeests from behind jump on top of them. Others are grabbed by crocodiles. Hundreds die—but most make it to the other side.

These blue wildebeests are all scrambling to get ⇒
out of the Mara River and up the hill. This is one of
the most dangerous parts of the migration.

Can We Learn More About Wildebeests?

If you are very lucky, you could go to Africa on a safari and watch the wildebeests migrate. Or perhaps a zoo near you keeps wildebeests. If you do see one in person, notice how graceful it is—even though its body looks so awkward! Lots of books and magazines have information on wildebeests, too.

Wildebeests are one of many fascinating animals that live on the African plains. Thanks to efforts to protect some of these areas, we can hope to see wildebeest herds galloping across the plains for centuries to come.

⟵ This adult blue wildebeest is standing in the afternoon sun, watching for danger.

Glossary

calves (KALVZ)
Baby wildebeests are called calves. Wildebeest calves learn to run soon after birth.

extinct (ek-STINKT)
When a kind of animal dies out completely, it is said to be extinct. Black wildebeests are extinct in the wild, but some are still alive in parks and zoos.

herds (HERDZ)
Herds are groups of animals that live together. Wildebeests live in large herds.

hooves (HOOVZ)
Hooves are hard, curved coverings over an animal's feet. Wildebeests have hooves.

mammals (MAM-mullz)
Mammals are animals that have hair or fur and feed their babies milk from their bodies. Wildebeests and people are mammals.

migrate (MY-grayt)
Animals migrate by moving from one location to another. Wildebeests migrate to find fresh grass and water.

predators (PRED-eh-terz)
Predators are animals that hunt and eat other animals. Many types of predators hunt wildebeests.

refuges (REF-yoo-jez)
Refuges are areas of land that are set aside for animals. Many wildebeests live in Africa's wildlife refuges.

Index

Web Sites

http://www.seaworld.org/animal_bytes/wildebeestab.html

http://www.planet-pets.com/plntwldb.htm

http://www.ultimateungulate.com/wtgnu.html